ABOUT THE OS

Flexbox Explained is part of the OSTraining Everything Club.

The club gives you access to all of the video classes, plus all the "Explained" books from OSTraining.

- These books are always up-to-date. Because we self-publish, we can release constant updates.

- These books are active. We don't do long, boring explanations.

- You don't need any experience. The books are suitable even for complete beginners.

Join the OSTraining Everything Club today by visiting our website at https://ostraining.com. You'll be able to download ebook copies of "Flexbox Explained" and all our other books and videos.

 OSTraining

ABOUT THE OSTRAINING TEAM

Stephen Burge has split his career between teaching and web development. In 2007, he combined the two by starting to teach web development. His company, OSTraining, now teaches web development training classes around the world and online. Stephen is originally from England, and now lives in Florida.

Jorge Montoya lived in Ecuador and Germany. Now he is back to his homeland Colombia. He spends his time translating from English and German to Spanish. He enjoys playing with Open Source Content Management Systems and technologies.

This book also would not be possible without the help of the OSTraining team.

Thanks to Steve's wife, Stacey. She has saved Steve from many mistakes over the years, and many terrible typos in this book.

WE OFTEN UPDATE THIS BOOK

This is version 1.0 of Flexbox Explained. This version was released on July 6, 2019.

We aim to keep this book up-to-date, and so regularly release new versions to keep up with changes in Flexbox.

ADVANTAGES AND DISADVANTAGES

We often release updates for this book. Most of the time, frequent updates are wonderful. If Flexbox makes a change in the morning, we can have a new version of this book available in the afternoon. Most traditional publishers wait years and years before updating their books.

There are two disadvantages to be aware of:

- Page numbers do change. We often add and remove material from the book to reflect changes in Flexbox.

- There's no index at the back of this book. This is because page numbers do change, and also because our self-publishing platform doesn't have a way to create indexes yet. We hope to find a solution for that soon.

Hopefully, you think that the advantages outweigh the disadvantages. If you have any questions, we're always happy to chat: books@ostraining.com.

ARE YOU AN AUTHOR?

If you enjoy writing about the web, we'd love to talk with you.

Most publishing companies are slow, boring, inflexible and don't pay very well.

Here at OSTraining, we try to be different:

- **Fun**: We use modern publishing tools that make writing books as easy as blogging.
- **Fast**: We move quickly. Some books get written and published in less than a month.
- **Flexible**: It's easy to update your books. If technology changes in the morning, you can update your book by the afternoon.
- **Fair**: Profits from the books are shared 50/50 with the author.

Do you have a topic you'd love to write about? We publish books on almost all web-related topics.

Whether you want to write a short 100-page overview, or a comprehensive 500-page guide, we'd love to hear from you.

Contact us via email: books@ostraining.com.

ARE YOU A TEACHER?

Many schools, colleges and organizations have adopted OSTraining books as teaching guides.

This book is designed to be a step-by-step guide that students can follow at different speeds. The book can be used for a one-day class, or a longer class over multiple weeks.

If you are interested in teaching Flexbox, we'd be delighted to help you with review copies, and all the advice you need.

Please email books@ostraining.com to talk with us.

SPONSOR AN OSTRAINING BOOK

Is your company interested in sponsoring an OSTraining book? Our books are some of the world's best-selling guides to the software they cover.

People love to read our books and learn about new web design topics.

Why not reach those people? Partner with us to showcase your company to thousands of web developers.
We have partnered with Acquia, Pantheon, Nexcess, GoDaddy, InMotion, GlowHost and Ecwid to provide sponsored training to millions of people.

If you want to learn more, visit https://ostraining.com/sponsor or email us at books@ostraining.com.

WE WANT TO HEAR FROM YOU

Are you satisfied with your purchase of Flexbox Explained? Let us know and help us reach others who would benefit from this book.

We encourage you to share your experience. Here are two ways you can help:

- Leave your review on Amazon's product page of Flexbox Explained.
- Email your review to books@ostraining.com.

Thanks for reading Flexbox Explained. We wish you the best in your future endeavors with Flexbox.

THE LEGAL DETAILS

CSS Flexbox Explained

CSS FLEXBOX EXPLAINED

Your Step-by-Step Guide to Flexbox

JORGE MONTOYA AND STEVE BURGE

OSTraining

CONTENTS

CHAPTER 1.

INTRODUCTION TO CSS FLEXBOX

Hi and welcome to CSS Flexbox. We're Jorge and Steve.

Over the last fifteen years, we've worked as web designers. It's been a fascinating time.

For many years, the most popular way to design websites was with frameworks such as Bootstrap and Foundation. We needed these frameworks because they added many features that we needed. The core features of CSS weren't enough for modern web development.

However, in recent years, the developers behind CSS worked to create "modules" including CSS Grid and Flexbox. These provide many of the features we need, but without requiring us to install anything.

You can use Flexbox simply by writing code in a file and opening your browser. That's what we're going to do throughout this book.

WHAT IS FLEXBOX?

Flexbox is a CSS module that gives you great flexibility when creating layouts.

What do we mean by "flexibility" here? Flexbox layouts can be organized top to bottom, bottom to top, left to right or right to left. This isn't the case with most layout tools.

Flexbox layouts have items (`flex-items`) inside a container (`flex-container`). These items can grow or shrink according to the available container space. The items "flex" to fit the parent container in the best possible way.

You can create a Flexbox layout in context by declaring a container using this property: `display : flex`

Flexbox uses a parent-child relationship so when you declare a flex container, the direct children of this container will automatically turn into flex items.

Flexbox is often confused with CSS Grid. Here's the key difference between Flexbox and CSS Grid:

- Flexbox is a one-dimensional layout model. It can manage either columns or rows.
- CSS Grid is a two-dimensional layout model. It can manage both columns and rows.

You can take a look at the official Flexbox W3C specification by visiting https://www.w3.org/TR/css-flexbox-1/.

If you're interested in CSS Grid, check out our book "CSS Grid Explained": https://www.ostraining.com/books/css-grid/.

HOW DOES FLEXBOX WORK?

Flexbox works on an axis grid.

In this book we're going to talk a lot about Flexbox properties. Every chapter will focus on a different property. Flexbox properties work either on the container or on the items, controlling how items are laid out inside your container.

Flex items can be laid out in all directions across their particular axis: left to right, right to left, top to bottom or bottom to top.

You can even change the order of the flex items without the need to alter the source order of your code.

Flex items can grow to fill the available space inside a container, or they can shrink to prevent overflow.

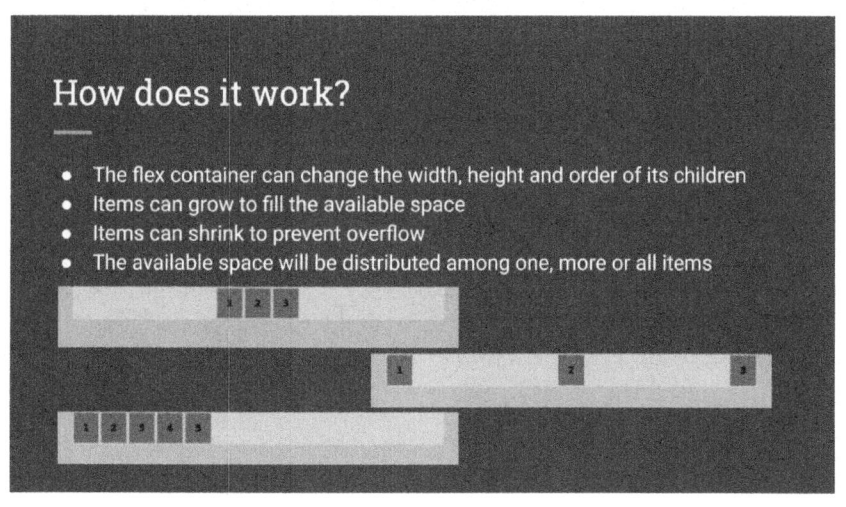

THE FLEXBOX AXES

A flexbox container has two axes:

- main axis
- cross axis

The main axis is determined by the value of the flex-direction property. The main axis can go in these directions:

- left to right: `flex-direction: row`
- right to left: `flex-direction: row-reverse`
- top to bottom: `flex-direction: column`
- bottom to top: `flex-direction: column-reverse`

The cross axis on the other side will always be perpendicular to the main axis. Take a look at the image below. This shows how the main axis is determined according to the different values of the flex-direction property.

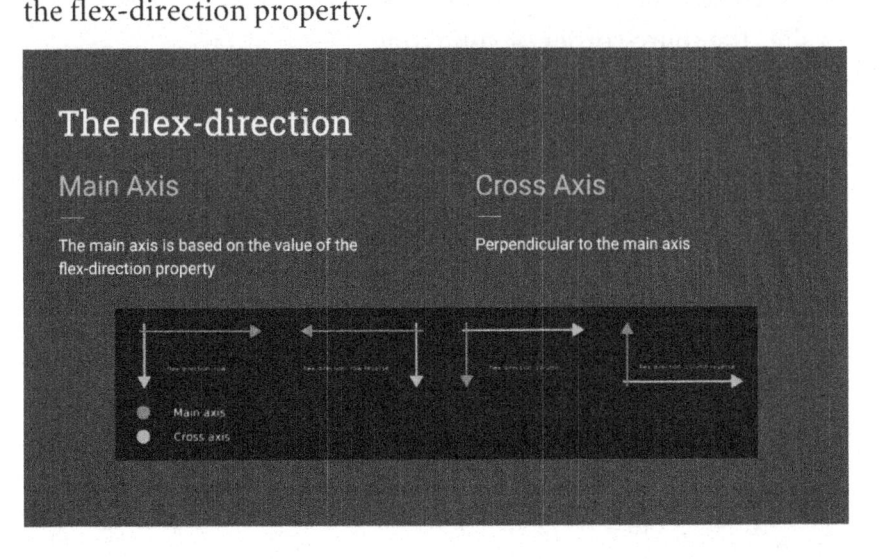

THE FLEXBOX PROPERTIES

The Flexbox module has its own set of properties. Some of these properties apply to the parent container while others apply to the flex items.

Properties for the parent	
`display`	Defines a flex container - flex formatting context
`flex-direction`	Defines the main axis inside the container
`flex-wrap`	Allows flex items to wrap onto more than one line
`flex-flow`	Shorthand for `flex-direction` + `flex-wrap`
`justify-content`	Aligns items along the main axis
`align-content`	Aligns items along the cross axis on a single line
`align-items`	Aligns multiple lines of items on the cross axis

Here are the properties for the child items:

Properties for the children

order	Allows to change the order of the items without altering the source order
flex-grow	An item can grow to fill up the available free space
flex-shrink	An item can shrink if there is not enough space available
flex-basis	Defines the size of an item before space is distributed
flex	Shorthand for flex-grow + flex-shrink + flex-basis
align-self	Ability to align one single item within the flex container

Come along with us and turn into a Flexbox user! In the next chapter, we'll build our first Flexbox layout.

CHAPTER 2.

CREATING YOUR FIRST FLEXBOX LAYOUT

In this chapter, we'll get you up-and-running with Flexbox.

For all the examples in this book, we have provided sample code for you to use. Follow along with the exercises and you'll learn how to use Flexbox!

CREATE THE HTML AND CSS

Let's start this example by creating an HTML file with some sample code. I've prepared some HTML for you – it's a container with three child elements.

- Open your preferred code editor.
- Create an empty HTML file called index.html.
- Copy the HTML code from here: https://codepen.io/ jorgemb76/pen/ErNaRx
- Paste that code in your HTML file.

Now that we have a container with three elements, let's add some styling.

- Create a CSS file called style.css.
- Place this file in the same folder as your HTML file.

- Add this code to style.css. You can copy-and-paste the code from here: https://codepen.io/jorgemb76/pen/ErNaRx.

```css
/* GLOBAL STYLES */
* {
box-sizing: border-box;
}

body {
background-color: #AAA;
margin: 0px 50px 50px;
}

/* Each item in the grid contains numbers */
.item {
padding: 2rem;
border: 5px solid #87b5ff;
border-radius: 3px;
font-size: 2em;
font-family: sans-serif;
font-weight: bold;
background-color: #1c57b5;
}
```

This image shows how your code will appear when you open the HTML file in a browser. The three child items are as wide as their parent container. The height is determined by the content of each item. Notice the padding of 2rem (about 32px on a desktop screen) on all sides.

THE CSS FLEXBOX STYLES

Now it's time to start the Flexbox portion of this tutorial.

- Edit the CSS file and add this code:

```
.container { display: flex; }
```

This image shows how your code will look now:

What has changed? On the technical side, the parent container is now a `flex-container`. The child elements have turned into `flex-items`.

Why has the size of the containers changed? The flex-items are not as wide as their parent container. They are now as wide as the content inside them. The `flex-items` appear as floated elements to the left. They behave like **inline** elements.

To clearly see the width of the parent container, you can apply a `background-color`:

- Edit the CSS code and add this code:

```
.container {
display: flex;
background-color: #f5ca3c;
}
```

Here's how the container now appears:

You already have noticed that the `flex-container` behaves (mostly) like a block-level element. However, we can also make the container behave like an inline-level element. To do this, we change the value of the `display` property to `inline-flex`.

- Edit the CSS code:

```
.container {
display: inline-flex;
background-color: #f5ca3c;
}
```

The flex container is now an inline-level element, as you can see in this image:

Before we continue, let's change the behavior to a block-level element.

- Edit the CSS code:

```
.container {
display: flex;
background-color: #f5ca3c;
flex-direction: row-reverse;
}
```

CHANGING FLEXBOX ROWS TO COLUMNS

So far, we've created a `flex-container`. We've also seen how the children of this container behave when turned into `flex-items`.

Now let's learn how to change the direction of our layout. The default direction of a `flex-container` is row-based. However, you can change this behavior with the `flex-direction` property.

- Edit the CSS code:

```
.container {
display: flex;
background-color: #f5ca3c;
flex-direction: row;
}
```

After updating your code, you will see no change because `flex-direction: row` is the default value. Let's make a really visible change: edit the direction of the `flex-container` to `column`.

- Edit the CSS code:

```
.container {
display: flex;
background-color: #f5ca3c;
flex-direction: column;
}
```

This next image shows the change in your layout:

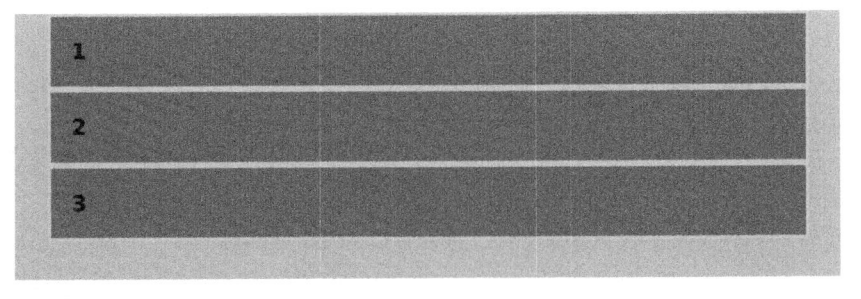

Now, the direction of the `flex-container` is based on the block axis (column). The `flex-items` are aligned from top to bottom, and each one of these items takes the full width of its parent container. So, they behave like block elements.

You may start to question things at this point: "Hey, my layout now *looks exactly the same as the very first layout in this tutorial!*" That's true. Visually, there's no difference between this current layout with a `flex-container` and the first layout of this example with a block container.

However, we now have more control. For example, you can invert the direction of `flex-items` with the `row-reverse` and `column-reverse` properties.

- Edit the CSS code:

```
.container {
display: flex;
background-color: #f5ca3c;
flex-direction: column-reverse;
}
```

To see the `flex-items` inverted in a row, change the value of the `flex-direction` property.

- Edit the CSS code:

```
.container {
display: flex;
background-color: #f5ca3c;
flex-direction: row-reverse;
}
```

CHAPTER SUMMARY

Congratulations! You have learned how to declare a `flex-container`. You have seen how `flex-items` behave depending on the `flex-direction` applied to their parent container (`row` or `column`). Also you know how to reverse the order of `flex-items`.

All these changes are done with CSS, so it will not affect the structure of the HTML markup of your site. That is one of the advantages of using Flexbox.

CHAPTER 3.

THE JUSTIFY-CONTENT PROPERTY

Now that you've built your first Flexbox layout, we're going to start looking at various Flexbox properties.

During the next ten chapters, we'll look at ten properties, with a detailed code example for each one.

In this chapter, we're going to introduce the `justify-content` property.

THE JUSTIFY-CONTENT PROPERTY

As you saw in the first chapter, the main axis of the `flex-container` is determined by the value of the `flex-direction` property. This image below shows how `flex-direction` controls the main axis and cross axis:

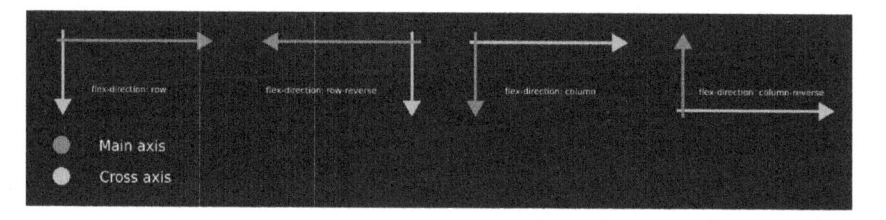

Understanding the main axis is important for this chapter because the `justify-content` property specifies how flex-items are distributed along the main axis.

This `justify-content` property has five different possible values:

1. `flex-start` (default)
2. `flex-end`
3. `center`
4. `space-between`
5. `space-around`

In the code examples for this chapter, we'll see all five of those values in action.

CREATE THE HTML AND CSS

- Open your preferred code editor.
- Create an empty HTML file.
- Copy this HTML code into your new file: https://codepen.io/jorgemb76/pen/pGGNoX.
- Create a CSS file called style.css.
- Add this CSS code, or copy it from the Codepen link above.

```
/* GLOBAL STYLES */
* {
box-sizing: border-box;
}

body {
background-color: #AAA;
margin: 0px 50px 50px;
}

.item {
padding: 2rem;
```

```
border: 5px solid #87b5ff;
border-radius: 3px;
font-size: 2em;
font-family: sans-serif;
font-weight: bold;
background-color: #1c57b5;
}

.container {
display: flex;
background-color: #f5ca3c;
flex-direction: column;
justify-content: space-around;
height: 90vh;
}
```

Once you've created the HTML and CSS, open the HTML in your browser. This is what you will see:

THE CSS FLEXBOX STYLES

We have our layout in place, so now it's time to add the Flexbox CSS:

- Edit the style.css file and add this code:

```
.container {
display: flex;
```

```
background-color: #f5ca3c;
}
```

What has happened here? The parent container has turned into a flex-container. The three children elements are now flex-items.

Next, let's use the `justify-content` property for the first time.

- Edit your CSS code:

```
.container {
display: flex;
background-color: #f5ca3c;
flex-direction: row;
justify-content: flex-start;
}
```

Has anything changed? No.

This is because default values for `flex-direction` and `justify-content` are `row` and `flex-start` respectively. We were already using the default values, so you won't see any changes in the layout when adding these properties. With default values, the main axis runs from left to right, whereas the cross axis runs from top to bottom.

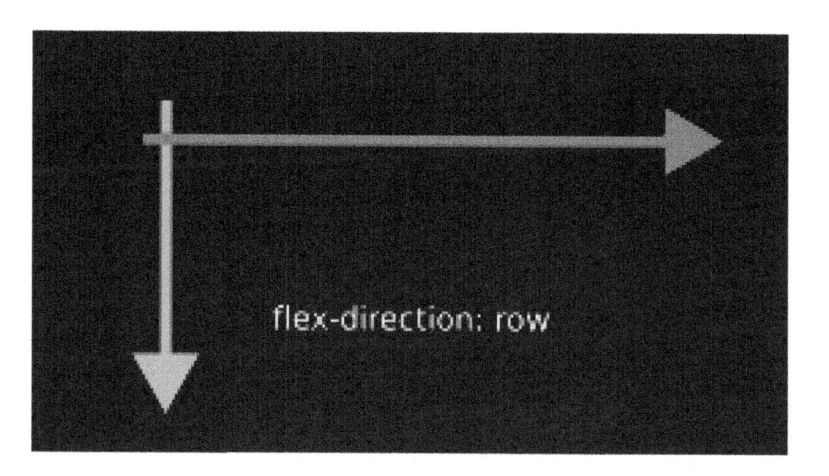

Now let's see a real change to our Flexbox layout. We're going to update the value of the `justify-content` property to `flex-end`.

- Edit the CSS code:

```
.container {
display: flex;
background-color: #f5ca3c;
flex-direction: row;
justify-content: flex-end;
}
```

This image shows your result. The flex-items are now placed at the end of the `flex-container`. The items run from left to right thanks to `flex-direction: row`.

Now we're going center the items within the `flex-container` by changing the value of the `justify-content` property again.

- Edit the CSS code:

```
.container {
display: flex;
background-color: #f5ca3c;
flex-direction: row;
justify-content: center;
}
```

Refresh your browser and your three items will be perfectly centered along the main axis of their parent container.

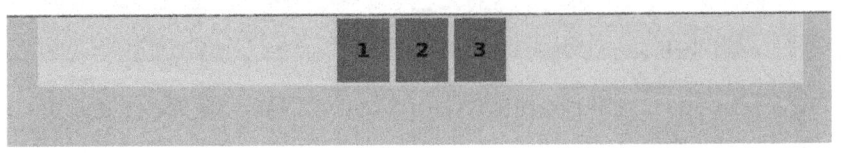

Let's change the value of the justify-content property once again.

- Edit the CSS code:

```
.container {
display: flex;
background-color: #f5ca3c;
flex-direction: row;
justify-content: space-between;
}
```

The available space is distributed between each one of the flex-items, thanks to justify-content: space-between. This means they are as far away from each other as possible, considering the full width of the container.

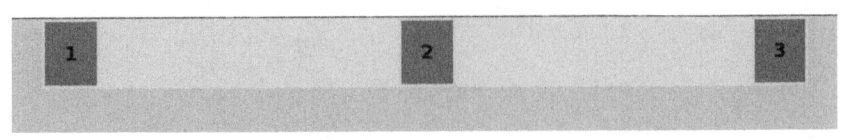

Now let's see the fifth value for the justify-content property.

- Edit the CSS code again:

```
.container {
display: flex;
background-color: #f5ca3c;
flex-direction: row;
justify-content: space-around;
}
```

In this case, the available space is distributed around the flex-items, so there is an even amount of space to the left and right of each flex-item.

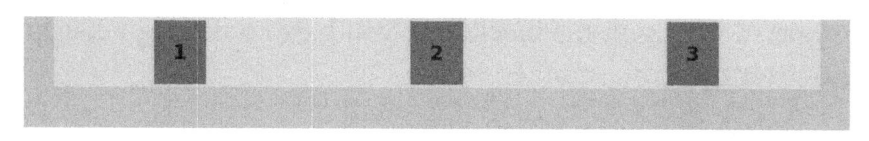

CHANGING FROM THE INLINE TO THE BLOCK AXIS

The `flex-direction` property determines whether the flex-items are distributed along the inline (row) or block (column) axis.

So far, we've only see flex-items distributed along the inline (row) axis.

To see the behavior of the items on the block axis, we'll make a few changes to the code.

- Edit the CSS file:

```
container {
display: flex;
background-color: #f5ca3c;
flex-direction: column;
justify-content: space-around;
}
```

Your flex-items are now stacked in a column:

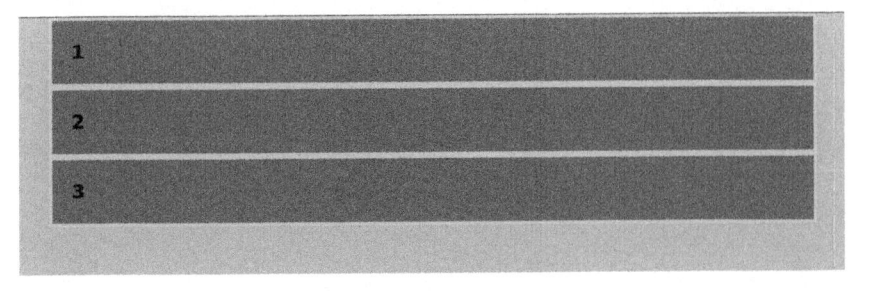

The flex-items behave now like block elements. That means they are as high as the content inside them. The same applies to the flex-container. In order to see how the justify-content property works on the block axis, you have to declare a height value for the flex-container.

- Edit the CSS code:

```
.container {
display: flex;
background-color: #f5ca3c;
flex-direction: column;
justify-content: space-around;
}
```

You can now see how justify-content: space-around; operates in a column:

CHAPTER SUMMARY

In this chapter, we looked at `justify-content` property and tested five values:

1. `flex-start` (default)
2. `flex-end`
3. `center`
4. `space-between`
5. `space-around`

We learned that the `justify-content` property specifies how flex-items are distributed along the main axis.

You might be able to guess what's coming in the next chapter. Turn the page and let's see how flex-items are distributed along the *cross* axis.

CHAPTER 4.

THE ALIGN-ITEMS PROPERTY

Earlier in this book, we learned that a flex-container has two axes:

- main axis
- cross axis

We've also seen that the `justify-content` property controls how the flex-items are distributed along the main axis.

In this chapter, we'll look at the `align-items` property, which controls how the flex-items are distributed along the cross axis.

Remember this chart from the previous chapter? It shows us the main axis, the cross axis and the `flex-direction` property.

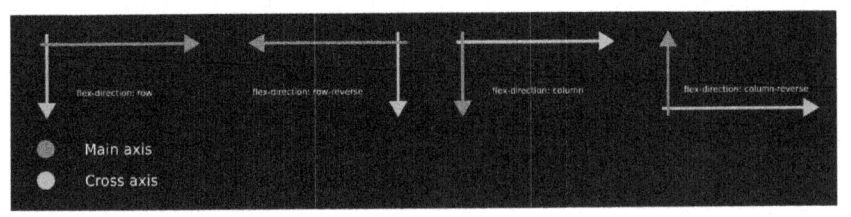

This chapter will introduce the `align-items` property and how to use it within a flex-container. The `align-items` property accepts five possible values:

1. `stretch` (default)

2. `flex-end`

3. `flex-start`

4. `center`

5. `baseline`

CREATE THE HTML AND CSS

- Open your preferred code editor.

- Create an empty HTML file.

- Copy the HTML code from this page: https://codepen.io/jorgemb76/pen/rRVEpp.

- Create a file called style.css.

- Add this code, or you can copy-and-paste it from the Codepen link above.

```css
/* GLOBAL STYLES */
* {
box-sizing: border-box;
}

body {
background-color: #AAA;
margin: 0px 50px 50px;
}

.item {
padding: 2rem;
border: 5px solid #87b5ff;
border-radius: 3px;
font-size: 2em;
font-family: sans-serif;
font-weight: bold;
background-color: #1c57b5;
}
```

Once your CSS and HTML is ready, this image shows what you'll see in your browser.

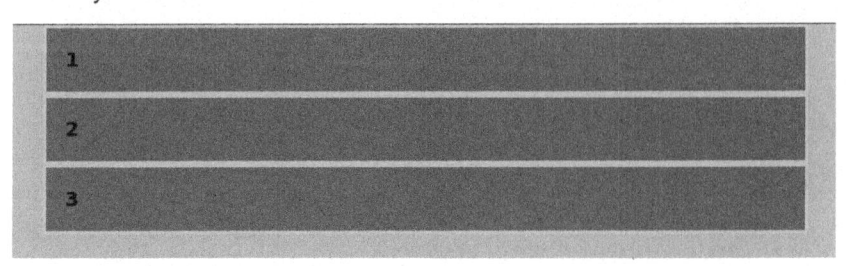

THE FLEXBOX STYLES

Let's start using Flebox in this chapter, and create a flex-container.

- Edit the CSS code:

```
.container {
display: flex;
background-color: #f5ca3c;
}
```

The image below shows what you'll see now. The defaults for flex-direction is row. The default for align-items is stretch. These defaults mean the main axis is the inline axis and the cross-axis is the block axis.

Let's specify the the align-items property for the first time.

- Update your CSS file:

```
.container {
display: flex;
background-color: #f5ca3c;
```

```
align-items: flex-end;
}
```

Refresh your browser and you will see no difference to the layout. This is because the flex-container is only as high as the items inside it, just like a regular block container.

In order to see how this works, you have to declare a height value for the flex-container.

- Edit the CSS code:

```
.container {
display: flex;
background-color: #f5ca3c;
height: 90vh;
align-items: flex-end;
}
```

In your browser, you'll see that the flex-items have been displaced to the end of the cross axis, thanks to the align-items property.

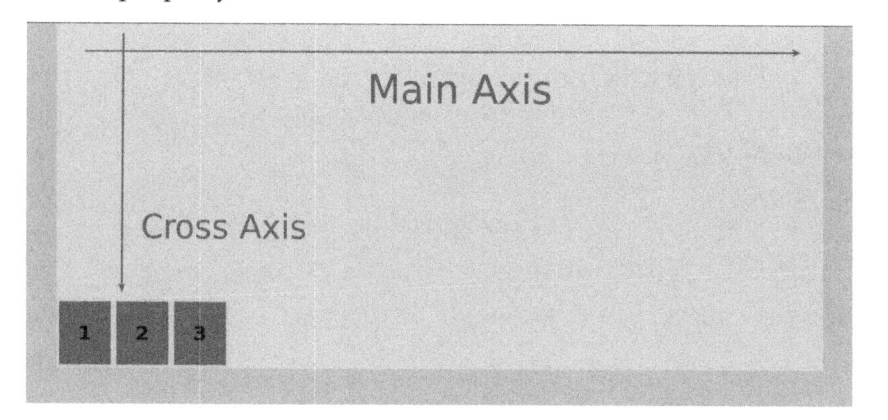

Let's test other possible values for the align-items property.

- Edit the CSS file:

```
.container {
```

```
display: flex;
background-color: #f5ca3c;
height: 90vh;
align-items: flex-start;
}
```

Now the flex-items are located at the start of both axes within the container. Remember that the default value for the justify-content property is flex-start and that the default value for the flex-direction property is row.

Let's try a third value for the align-items property.

- Edit the CSS file once again:

```
.container {
display: flex;
background-color: #f5ca3c;
height: 90vh;
align-items: center;
}
```

The items are now vertically centered along the cross axis:

If you want to center the items perfectly within the container, you just add the `justify-content` property with the value `center`.

- Edit the CSS code:

```
.container {
display: flex;
background-color: #f5ca3c;
height: 90vh;
align-items: center;
justify-content: center;
}
```

Now your items are truly in the center of the container:

- Edit the CSS code to remove the `justify-content` property and the `align-items` property.

```
.container {
display: flex;
background-color: #f5ca3c;
height: 90vh;
}
```

Refresh your browser, and your items will be on the left of the container.

Why are the items so tall? Remember that the default value for the `align-items` property is `stretch`. Remember also that if you edit the code and add this default value property, you will see no difference when compared to not including the property.

- For example, change your CSS to the following code:

```
.container {
display: flex;
background-color: #f5ca3c;
height: 90vh;
align-items: stretch;
}
```

Now change the font-size of two of the flex-items.

- Edit the CSS code:

```
.item2 {
font-size: 3em;
}

.item3 {
font-size: 3.5em;
}
```

The image below shows what you will see in your browser. I've added the red, brown and green lines to make it easier to see the bottom of each flex-item.

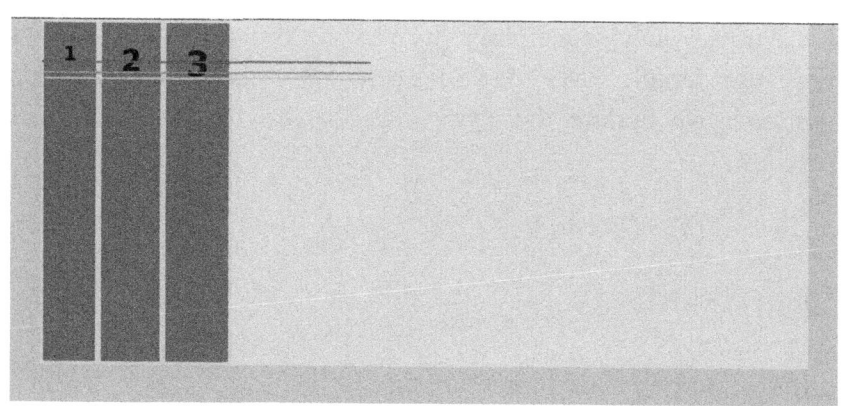

You'll notice that the baselines of the flex-items do not align with each other. In order to align all the items, according to their baseline, we must assign the baseline value to the align-items property.

- Edit the CSS code:

```
.container {
display: flex;
background-color: #f5ca3c;
height: 90vh;
align-items: baseline;
}
```

This next image shows the result. Again, I've added an extra line so you can see the base-line of each item:

Until now, you have seen how the `align-items` property works with the default `flex-direction: row`. Let's see how this works if we update the `flex-direction` to use a value of `column`.

- Edit the CSS code:

```
.container {
display: flex;
background-color: #f5ca3c;
flex-direction: column;
align-items: center;
}
```

Your items will now be stacked vertically. Notice that you don't have to declare a height value for the container since the main-axis is now the block axis.

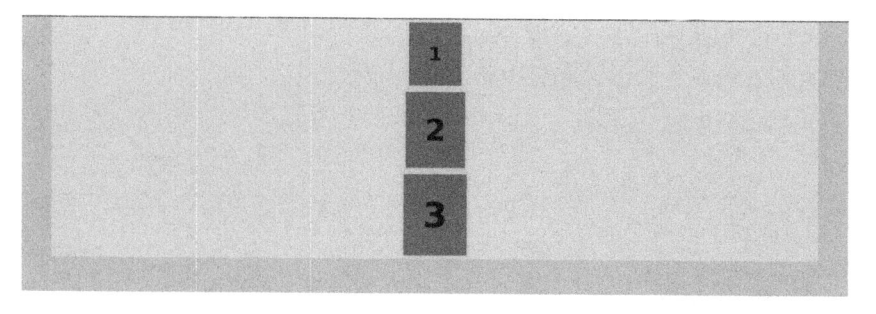

Let's keep experimenting. What happens if the `align-items` property has a value of `flex-end`?

- Edit the CSS code:

```
.container {
display: flex;
background-color: #f5ca3c;
flex-direction: column;
align-items: flex-end;
}
```

Your items will now be stacked on the right side of the container:

You might be able to guess what happens if the `align-items` property has a value of `flex-start`. But, let's update the code and see the change.

- Edit the CSS code:

```
.container {
display: flex;
```

```
background-color: #f5ca3c;
flex-direction: column;
align-items: flex-start;
}
```

CHAPTER SUMMARY

In this chapter, we've explored the five possible values for the `align-items` property:

1. `stretch` (default)
2. `flex-end`
3. `flex-start`
4. `center`
5. `baseline`

Over the last two chapters, we've learned that, the `align-items` property works always on the cross-axis, while the `justify-content` property works always on the main-axis.

In the next chapter, we'll see how items can grow or shrink along the main axis.

CHAPTER 5.

THE FLEX-GROW PROPERTY

The previous two chapters were a closely-connected pair:

- the `justify-content` property controls how the flex-items are distributed along the main axis.

- the `align-items` property which controls how the flex-items are distributed along the cross axis.

The same is true of the next two chapters:

- The `flex-grow` property specifies how items will grow along the main axis.

- The `flex-shrink` property specifies how items will shrink if there's not enough space available.

In this chapter, we'll take you though examples of how to use the `flex-grow` property.

CREATE THE HTML AND CSS

- Open your preferred code editor.

- Create an empty HTML file.

- Copy this HTML code into your new file:
  https://codepen.io/jorgemb76/pen/VRQyQX.

- Create a file called style.css.
- Add the following CSS code or take it from the Codepen link above:

```css
/* GLOBAL STYLES */
* {
box-sizing: border-box;
}

body {
background-color: #AAA;
margin: 0px 50px;
}

.item {
padding: 2rem;
border: 5px solid #87b5ff;
border-radius: 3px;
font-size: 2em;
font-family: sans-serif;
font-weight: bold;
background-color: #1c57b5;
}
```

Once your HTML and CSS files are set up correctly, this is what you'll see in your browser:

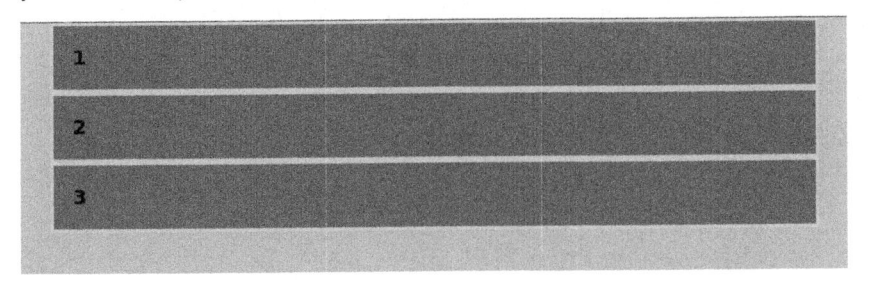

THE CSS FLEXBOX STYLES

Let's get started by declaring the parent container as the `flex` container.

- Edit the CSS code:

```
.container {
display: flex;
background-color: #f5ca3c;
}
```

The flex-items automatically position themselves into the `flex` container, as if they were inline elements. However, this doesn't fit every use-case. For example, you will often want to use all the available space in the `flex` container. You might also want to set the different items to be different sizes.

In our first `flex-grow` example, let's suppose that the second item has to be twice as wide as the first and third items.

- Edit the CSS file:

```
.item1 {
flex-grow: 1;
}

.item2 {
flex-grow: 2;
}

.item3 {
flex-grow: 1;
}
```

This image shows what happens now that the second item is twice as wide as the others.

If you resize your browser window, you'll notice that the second item will keep this proportion, if there's enough space available considering the width of the viewport. The image below shows the same layout but at a width of 768px.

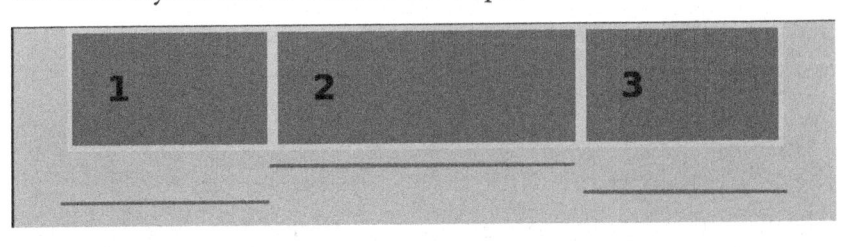

The image below shows the same layout at a width of 375px, the second item does not have enough space in the container to be twice as wide as the other two items, considering the content inside them. So the available space is distributed equally between all three items.

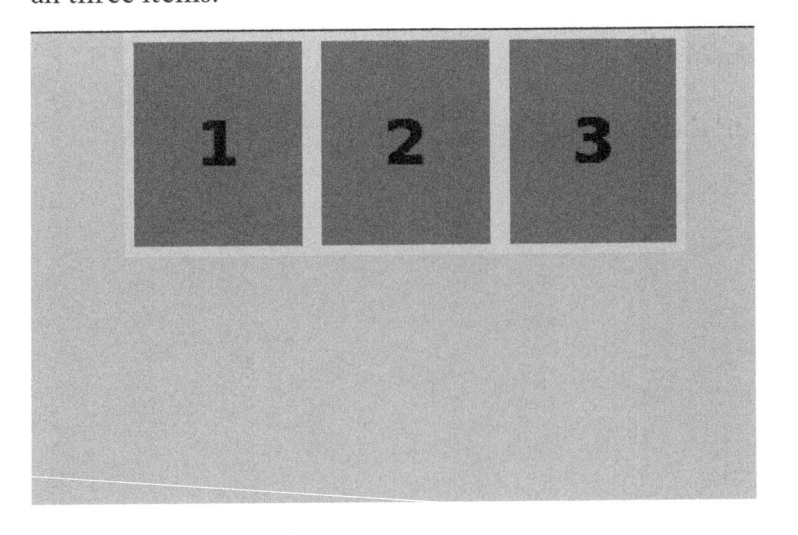

Flex-grow in Column Based Layout

When working on the block axis, it is important to remember that the height of items is set to `auto` by default. This means that each flex-item is only as high as the content inside it.

In order to test the `flex-grow` property on the block axis, we have to declare a fixed height for the `flex` container.

- Edit the CSS code:

```
.container {
display: flex;
background-color: #f5ca3c;
flex-direction: column;
height: 90vh;
}
```

The second item is now twice as high as the other two items, according to the available vertical space within the `flex` container. This makes sense if you have a fixed design and you know the exact size of the content. Please note that the `flex-grow` property will not work if the content inside an item is higher than the height you've specified for that item.

Let's see how our new layout works with some dummy *lore ipsum dolor* content:

- Edit the HTML code:

```
<div class="container">
<div class="item item1">1</div>
<div class="item item2">Lorem ipsum dolor sit
amet consectetur adipisicing elit. Consequuntur
eos dolores impedit nulla delectus illo dolorum
quas, laudantium voluptatem iusto ab tempore
porro, earum aliquid debitis repudiandae magni
aperiam reiciendis natus odit explicabo. Ut
deleniti ea autem voluptatem, explicabo neque
modi atque recusandae commodi molestiae quasi
itaque repellat similique debitis pariatur
aliquid ipsam soluta error doloremque ab quas.
Soluta, nemo!</div>
<div class="item item3">3</div>
</div>
```

CHAPTER SUMMARY

In this chapter, we've seen that the `flex-grow` property allows you distribute the available space in the `flex` container between all flex-items inside it.

However, sometimes your layout will not have enough space and your items will need to adapt. In the next chapter, you'll see how that's done with the `flex-shrink` property.

CHAPTER 6.

THE FLEX-SHRINK PROPERTY

As you saw in the last chapter, the `flex-grow` property specifies how items expand to fill the available space in your flex-container.

In contrast, the `flex-shrink` property specifies how items behave when there's not enough space available for all of them to fit.

The default value for `flex-shrink` is 1. This means that all items shrink in an equal proportion.

Let's demonstrate the `flex-shrink` property with some examples.

CREATE THE HTML AND CSS

- Open your preferred code editor.
- Create an empty HTML file.
- Copy this code: https://codepen.io/jorgemb76/pen/zbgvyW.
- Create a file called *style.css*.
- Add following code or copy-and-paste it from the Codepen above:

```
/* GLOBAL STYLES */
* {
box-sizing: border-box;
}

body {
background-color: #AAA;
margin: 0px 50px 50px;
}

.item {
padding: 2rem;
border: 5px solid #87b5ff;
border-radius: 3px;
font-size: 2em;
font-family: sans-serif;
font-weight: bold;
background-color: #1c57b5;
}
```

THE CSS FLEXBOX STYLES

Let's declare the parent container as a flex-container.

- Edit the CSS code:

```
.container {
display: flex;
background-color: #f5ca3c;
}
```

The parent container is a flex-container now and its children have turned into flex-items.

Go back to your code editor and change the width of the parent container to 600px.

- Edit the CSS file:

```css
.container {
display: flex;
background-color: #f5ca3c;
width: 600px;
}
```

This next image shows what happens to your layout:

Next, change the width of the items to 250px each. If you do the math, you can realize that three 250px items are not going to fit into a 600px container.

- Edit the CSS file:

```css
.item {
width: 250px;
}
```

Despite the fact that you declared each item to be 250px wide, items cannot overflow the width of their parent. So each item will shrink to 200px. This happens because the default behavior is `flex-shrink: 1` which causes all the items to shrink in the same proportion.

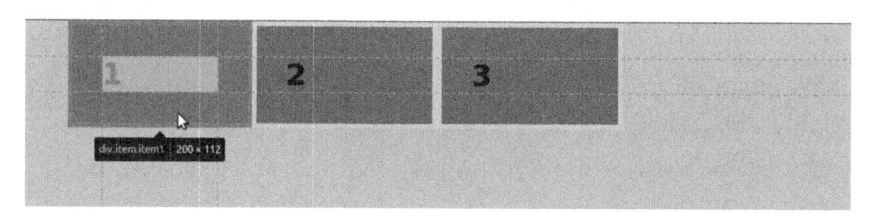

Let's add the `flex-shrink` property to our code. In this first taksk, we'll add the default value to the first item for checking purposes.

- Edit the CSS file:

```
.item1 {
flex-shrink: 1;
}
```

Refresh your browser and your layout remains unchanged.

Now change the value of the `flex-shrink` property for the first item once again.

- Edit the CSS file:

```
.item1 {
flex-shrink: 2;
}
```

The first item has reduced its width to 175px. The 25px "available space" left free are taken proportionally by the other two items.

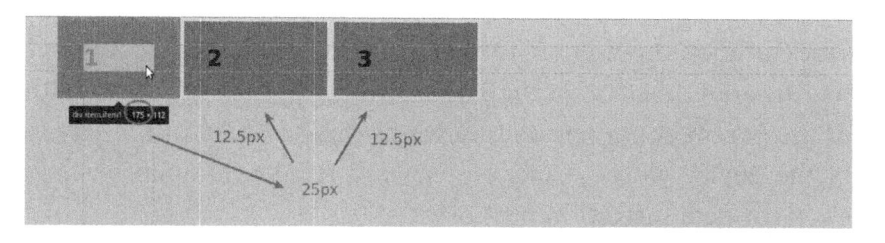

Now change the width of the parent container to 500px.

- Edit the CSS file:

```css
.container {
display: flex;
background-color: #f5ca3c;
width: 500px;
}
```

The difference between the first item and other two is now more noticeable. Item #1 is now only 125px wide.

I wonder what happens if we give an item a `flex-shrink` value of 0?

- Edit the CSS file:

```css
.item1 {
flex-shrink: 0;
}
```

Item #3 did not shrink at all, whereas Items #1 and #2 have to share the available space left in the container. Item #1 shrinks twice as far as Item #2 because of the `flex-shrink` property.

One thing we should note in closing is that specifying a container width is not practical in the real world. This is because the width of the parent container does depends on the width of the screen of the device you're using. However, a fixed container width is good for demonstration purposes.

CHAPTER SUMMARY

The `flex-shrink` property is the opposite of the the `flex-grow` property that we covered in the last chapter.

The `flex-shrink` property specifies how items behave when there's not enough space available for all of them to fit.

The next chapter will introduce the `flex-basis` property, which sets the initial width of the flex-items. Using the `flex-basis` property, you can combine `flex-grow, flex-shrink` and `flex-basis` in one shorthand to obtain better results.

CHAPTER 7.

THE FLEX-BASIS PROPERTY

In the last two chapters, we introduced two Flexbox properties. Each of those properties have an opposite effect on items in a flex container:

- The `flex-grow` property specifies how items expand.
- The `flex-shrink` property specifies how items contract.

In this chapter, we look at the `flex-basis` property which sets the initial length of the flex-items inside a flex-container.

You can think of it as an improved version of the `width` or `height` values. The `flex-basis` has always prevalence over `width` or `height`.

CREATE THE HTML AND CSS

- Open your preferred code editor.
- Create an empty HTML file.
- Copy this code to your new file: https://codepen.io/jorgemb76/pen/dLLjbM.
- Create a file called style.css.
- Add the following CSS code, or copy it from the Codepen

above.

```
/* GLOBAL STYLES */
* {
box-sizing: border-box;
}

body {
background-color: #AAA;
margin: 0px 50px 50px;
}

.item {
padding: 2rem;
border: 5px solid #87b5ff;
border-radius: 3px;
font-size: 2em;
font-family: sans-serif;
font-weight: bold;
background-color: #1c57b5;
}
```

Open your browser and you should see this layout:

THE CSS FLEXBOX STYLES

You've done this a few times already in this book: declare the parent container as a flex container.

- Edit the CSS code:

```
.container {
display: flex;
background-color: #f5ca3c;
}
```

Now let's set the width of each flex-item to 33.33%. This allows our items to cover the whole flex-container area.

- Edit the CSS code:

```
.item {
width: 33.33%;
}
```

Each one of the items takes one-third of the whole container width.

Let's put the `flex-basis` property into action:

- Edit the CSS code:

```
.item {
flex-basis: 25%;
width: 33.33%;
}
```

Each item now has a width of 25% rather than 33.33%. Notice that I put the `flex-basis` declaration before the `width` declaration. I did this in order to demonstrate that `flex-basis` has **always** prevalence over `width`.

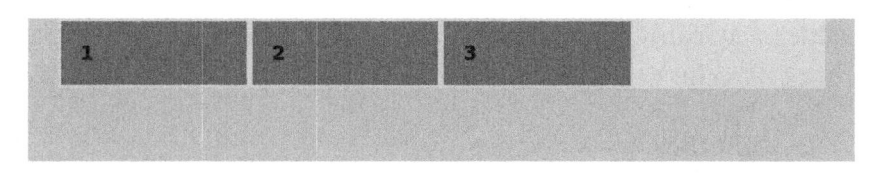

Our flex-container has a width of `1266px` on a common laptop screen. Let's change the width of the flex-container to `810px` and the flex-basis of each flex-item to `300px`.

- Edit the CSS code:

```
.container {
display: flex;
background-color: #f5ca3c;
width: 810px;
}

.item {
flex-basis: 300px;
}
```

Refresh your layout and the three items have a width of 270px.

Question: Can you work out what's happened here?

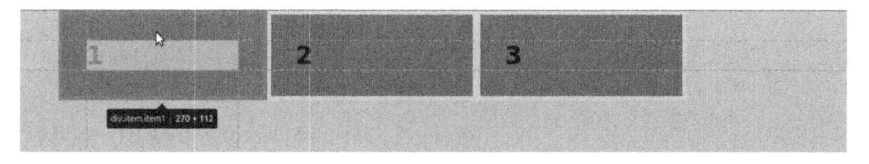

Answer: The key to this layout is that the `flex-basis` property refers to an ideal size of the flex-items. The `flex-basis` property applies only if there is enough space available in the flex-container. Our flex-items were declared with a `flex-basis` value of `300px`, but the flex-container is not wide enough, so each flex-item can only be `270px` wide.

Flex-items will grow and/or shrink past their `flex-basis`

value, according to their `flex-grow` and/or `flex-shrink` property values.

- Edit the CSS code once again:

```
.item {
max-width: 150px;
flex-basis: 300px;
}
```

The `max-width` value acts in this case as an upper limit of the `flex-basis` property. That means flex-items are not allowed to be wider than 150px, although the `flex-basis` property value was set to 300px.

Let's see a similar result with the `min-width` value.

- Edit the CSS code:

```
.item {
min-width: 200px;
flex-basis: 150px;
}
```

The `min-width` value acts in this case as a lower limit of the `flex-basis` property.

The flex-basis Property on the Block Axis

So far in this chapter, we've seen the `flex-basis` property acting on the width of flex-items on the inline axis.

On the block axis (`flex-direction: column`), the `flex-basis` property takes the height of the flex-items into account, instead of their width.

- Edit the CSS code:

```css
.container {
display: flex;
flex-direction: column;
background-color: #f5ca3c;
}

.item {
flex-basis: 150px;
height: 200px;
}
```

Your items will now be stacked in a column layout. In this case, the `flex-basis` value prevails over the `height` value, just like with the `width` value on the inline axis.

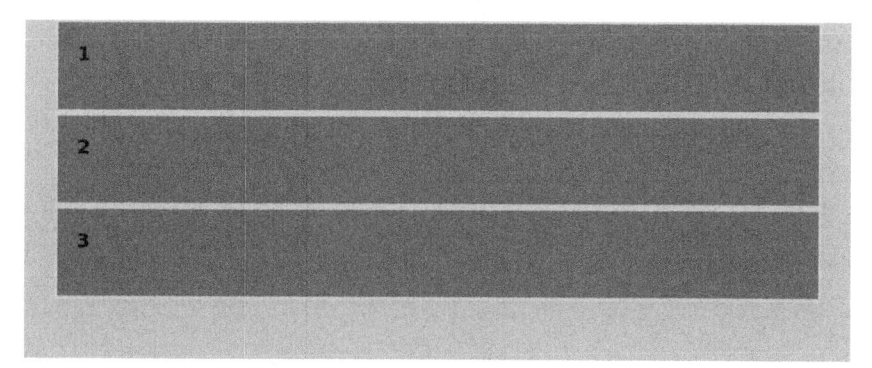

Let's update our code with the `min-height` value.

- Edit the CSS code:

```css
.item {
min-height: 200px;
flex-basis: 150px;
}
```

The `min-height` property acts in as the lower limit of the `flex-basis` property so the `height` of the flex-items will not be less than `200px`. The `min-height` value is acting independently of the value of the `flex-basis` property.

What happens if the `max-height` value is less than the `flex-basis` value?

- Edit the CSS code:

```
.item {
max-height: 150px;
flex-basis: 250px;
}
```

As you can see, the `max-height` value is the important value, and the `flex-basis` value is ignored.

Let's see how our layout looks with some *lore ipsum dolor* dummy text.

- Edit the HTML code:

```
<div class="container">
<div class="item item1">Lorem ipsum, dolor sit
amet consectetur adipisicing elit. Natus eaque
```

```
ducimus inventore provident possimus culpa quas
fugiat    voluptatibus    officiis    cupiditate!
Laboriosam  architecto,  dolorum  ad  voluptatum
veniam quibusdam nam vero ipsa cumque magnam sint
alias officiis.</div>
<div class="item item2">2</div>
<div class="item item3">3</div>
</div>
```

- Edit the CSS code:

```
.item {
max-height: 200px;
flex-basis: 125px;
}
```

What has happened in the image above? The height of the first item is 200px because that's the upper limit of the flex-basis property. However, the height of the other two flex-items is 125px because that's the declared value of flex-basis.

CHAPTER SUMMARY

This chapter built on what we learned in the last two chapters about the flex-grow and flex-shrink properties.

The flex-basis property specifies the initial size of flex-items before the available space inside the flex-container is distributed according to the flex factors (`flex-grow` and/or `flex-shrink`).

In the next chapter, we'll move on from talking about the size of items, and learn about ordering items in Flexbox.

CHAPTER 8.

THE ORDER PROPERTY

Flexbox doesn't only provide us ways to control the direction and size of items in our layout. Flexbox also enables us to control the order of items, thanks to the order property.

If you want to place flex-items in a particular sequence inside their flex-container, independently of how they are placed in the HTML code, you use the order property.

Back at the beginning of the book, we saw how to invert the order of the flex-items using row-reverse on the inline axis. This is useful when using right-to-left languages like Urdu or Hebrew. This image shows row-reverse and other values for the flex-direction property.

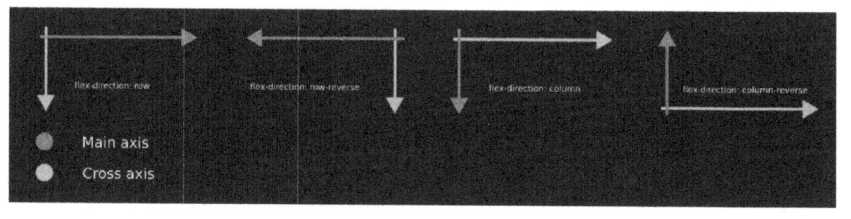

The order property gives you much more flexibility because it allows you to **visually** change the order of each item and still keep the source order in the HTML code. This is very useful for people who use screen readers. If a visitor is browsing your site with a screen reader, they will hear the items in the order they are placed in your HTML code.

CREATE THE HTML AND CSS

- Open your preferred code editor.
- Create an empty HTML file.
- Copy this HTML code: https://codepen.io/jorgemb76/pen/wbvjGd.

We have a container with five elements, each one of these is numbered in a logical order in the HTML markup. Let's add some basic styling.

- Create an empty CSS file and call it *style.css.*
- Write this code, or take it from the Codepen link above.

```css
/* GLOBAL STYLES */
* {
box-sizing: border-box;
}

body {
background-color: #AAA;
margin: 0px 50px 50px;
}

.item {
padding: 2rem;
border: 5px solid #87b5ff;
border-radius: 3px;
font-size: 2em;
font-family: sans-serif;
font-weight: bold;
background-color: #1c57b5;
}
```

THE CSS FLEXBOX STYLES

Let's start by declaring the container as a flex-container:

- Edit the CSS code.

```
.container {
display: flex;
background-color: #f5ca3c;
}
```

The default value for the `order` property is 0.

- Edit the CSS code:

```
.item2 {
order: 0;
}
```

As you can see, Item #2 is still in the same position. If the value for the `order` property is 0, your items won't move.

If you assign an item an `order` value greater than 0, it will place itself at the end, according to the `flex-direction` value.

- Edit the CSS code:

```
.item2 {
order: 1;
}
```

Now you'll see that Item #2 has moved to the final position:

Can you guess what happens if you assign an item an `order` value less than 0?

The answer is it will place itself at the beginning, according the the `flex-direction` value.

- Edit the CSS code to update Item #4:

```
.item4 {
order: -1;
}
```

Item #4 is now at the beginning of our items:

Items #1, #3 and #5 in our layout still have a default `order` value of 0, so they appear next to each other, taking into account their order in the source code (HTML). Despite the visual appearance of the layout, a screen reader will start with Item #1, because that is the order in the HTML markup.

On the Block Axis

In order to see how this property works on the block axis, add the `flex-direction` property with the value `column` to the flex-container.

- Edit the CSS code:

```
.container {
display: flex;
background-color: #f5ca3c;
flex-direction: column;
}
```

Refresh your layout in the browser, and this is what you'll see:

CHAPTER SUMMARY

The `order` property allows you to change the visual order of flex-items, without the need of changing the order of them in the HTML markup. This allows you to preserve the logical order of your site for accessibility and screen readers, while still have the freedom to arrange the layout of your site as you wish.

CHAPTER 9.

THE FLEX-WRAP PROPERTY

Until now, you have seen that flex-items stay on the same line. We have changed their size, their direction, and their order. However, our items have always remained on the same line.

With the `flex-wrap` property, it is possible to make flex-items wrap over to the next line.

CREATE THE HTML AND CSS

- Open your preferred code editor.
- Create an empty HTML file.
- Copy the HTML code from here: https://codepen.io/jorgemb76/pen/qGPVrO.
- Create an empty CSS file and call it style.css.
- Add this code to the file, or borrow it from the Codepen link above.

```
/* GLOBAL STYLES */
* {
box-sizing: border-box;
}

body {
background-color: #AAA;
```

```
margin: 0px 50px 50px;
}

.item {
padding: 2rem;
border: 5px solid #87b5ff;
border-radius: 3px;
font-size: 2em;
font-family: sans-serif;
font-weight: bold;
background-color: #1c57b5;
}
```

When you open your HTML file in your browser, this is what you'll see:

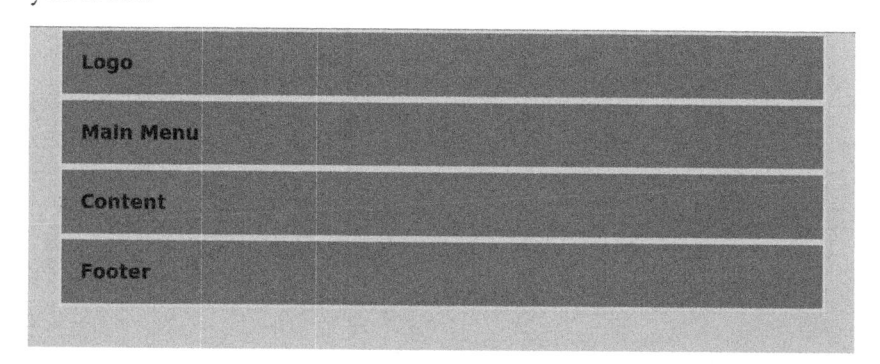

THE CSS FLEXBOX STYLES

Let's declare the main container as a flex-container.

- Edit the CSS code:

```
.container {
display: flex;
background-color: #f5ca3c;
}
```

This image shows how your layout appears with Flexbox added. Each flex-item is now as wide as the content inside it.

Let's declare the "width" of each flex-item, based on the `flex-basis` property that we covered earlier in the book.

- Edit the CSS code:

```
.item1 {
flex-basis: 50%;
}

.item2 {
flex-basis: 50%;
}

.item3 {
flex-basis: 80%;
}

.item4 {
flex-basis: 100%;
}
```

Each item has now a predefined width, and those widths add up to 280%, but the items still stay on the same line. This is where the `flex-wrap` property is useful.

Let's add the `flex-wrap` property.

- Edit the CSS code:

```
.container {
```

```
display: flex;
background-color: #f5ca3c;
flex-wrap: wrap;
}
```

Your layout is now updated and each item is sized correctly, according to the `flex-basis` widths.

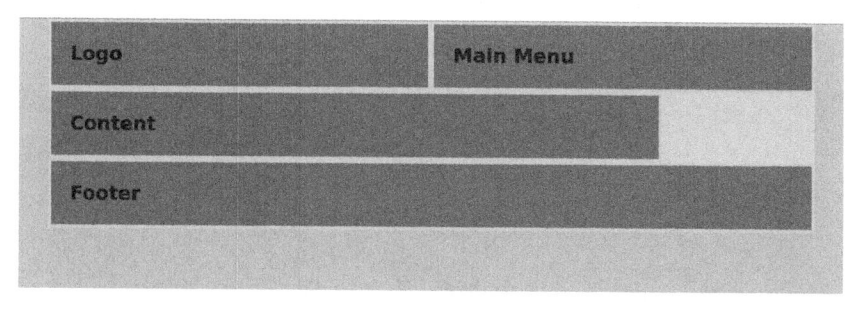

Let's center the "Content" item on the main axis.

- Edit the CSS code:

```
.item3 {
flex-basis: 80%;
margin: auto;
}
```

The `flex-wrap` property has two other possible values:

- `nowrap` which is the default value.
- `wrap-reverse` which inverts the order of start and end on the cross axis.

Let's update the CSS code with the `wrap-reverse` value:

```
.container {
display: flex;
background-color: #f5ca3c;
flex-wrap: wrap-reverse;
}
```

The items in your layout are now loading in reverse oder:

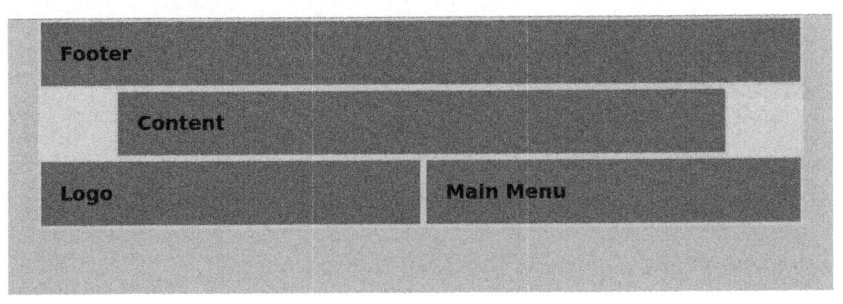

CHAPTER SUMMARY

The `flex-wrap` property allows you to wrap items onto the next line, that way you have control over the placement of flex-items and can easily achieve your desired layout.

There are three possible values for the `flex-wrap` property:

- `nowrap` which is the default value.
- `nowrap` which moves items onto the next line when they run out of space.
- `wrap-reverse` which inverts the order of start and end on the cross axis.

In the next chapter, we'll build on our knowledge of the `flex-wrap` property and take more control over the extra rows in our layouts.

CHAPTER 10.

THE ALIGN-CONTENT PROPERTY

Earlier in this book, you learned that the `align-items` flexbox property specifies how flex-items are distributed along the cross axis of the flex-container.

In the last chapter, you saw the `flex-wrap` property.

We're now going to build on both of those earlier lessons with the `align-content` property,

The `align-content` property specifies how the lines inside the container will be distributed once you have applied the `flex-wrap` property.

The `align-content` property accepts six possible values:

- `stretch` (default)
- `center`
- `flex-start`
- `flex-end`
- `space-between`
- `space-around`

CREATE THE HTML AND CSS

- Open your preferred code editor.

- Create an empty HTML file.

- Copy this HTML into your file: https://codepen.io/jorgemb76/pen/mYXgxM.

- Create a file called style.css.

- Add this code, or copy it from the Codepen link above.

```css
/* GLOBAL STYLES */ {
box-sizing: border-box;
}

body {
background-color: #AAA;
margin: 0px 50px 50px;
}

.item {
padding: 2rem;
border: 5px solid #87b5ff;
border-radius: 3px;
font-size: 2em;
font-family: sans-serif;
font-weight: bold;
background-color: #1c57b5;
}
```

This is how your initial layout will look:

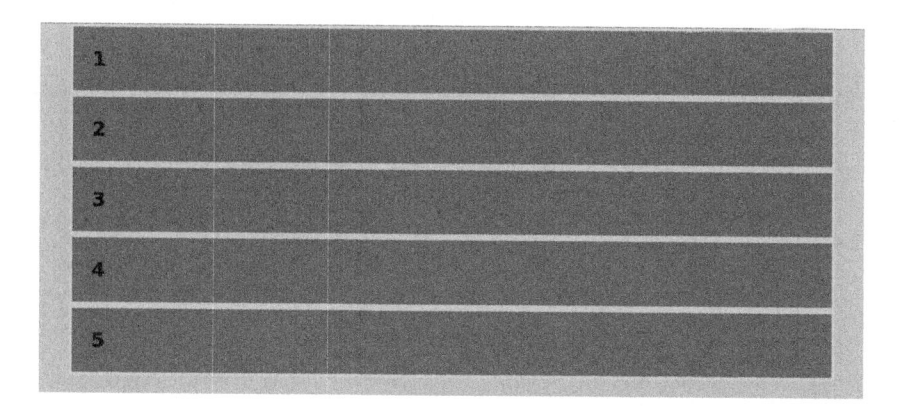

THE FLEXBOX STYLES

Let's declare the flex-container and get the Flexbox ball rolling:

- Edit the CSS code:

```
.container {
display: flex;
background-color: #f5ca3c;
}
```

Each one of the items inside the container is a flex-item now. In order to generate multiple lines, we will wrap the items with the help of the flex-wrap property at the container level. Furthermore, you have to change the width of the flex-items based on the value of the flex-basis property.

- Edit the CSS code:

```
.container {
display: flex;
background-color: #f5ca3c;
flex-wrap: wrap;
}
```

```
.item {
flex-basis: 50%;
}
```

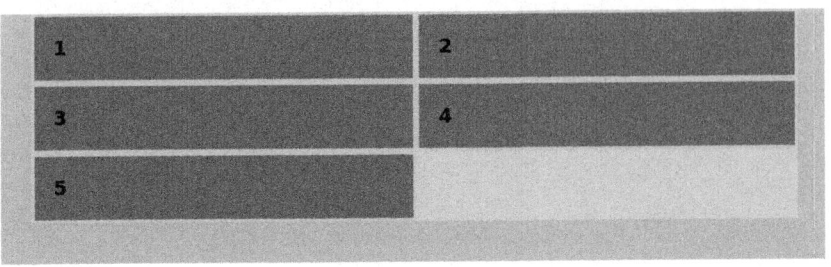

The height of the flex-container is determined by the total height of the items inside them. In order to demonstrate the align-content property, it is necessary to assign the main container a fixed height value.

- Edit the CSS code:

```
.container {
display: flex;
background-color: #f5ca3c;
flex-wrap: wrap;
height: 100vh;
}
```

The flex-container is now as high as the viewport screen.

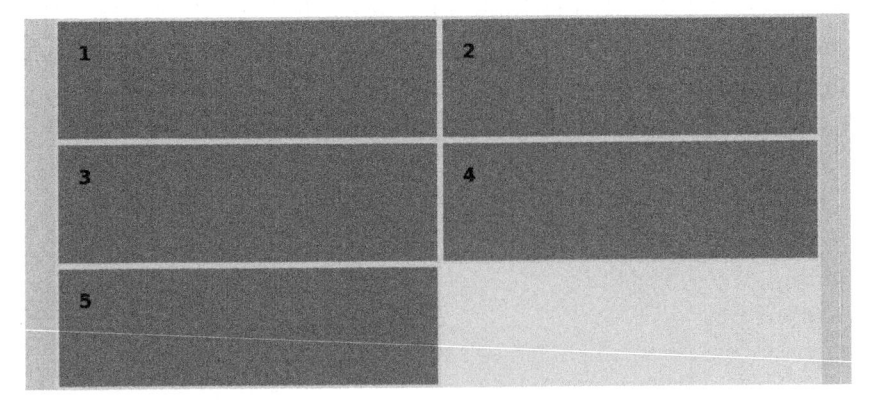

Let's test some different values for the `align-content` property:

- Edit the CSS code.

```css
.container {
display: flex;
background-color: #f5ca3c;
flex-wrap: wrap; height: 100vh;
align-content: center;
}
```

Remember that `align-content` refers to the wrapped lines and not to the items. In this case, the three lines of the layout have been placed at the center of the flex-container.

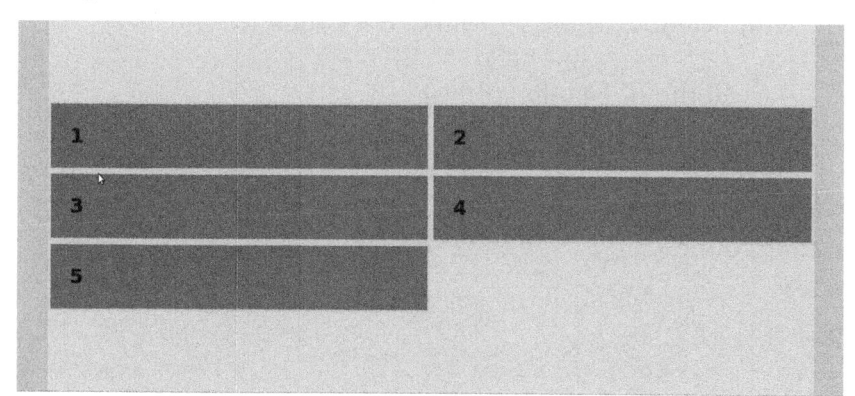

Let's test the `flex-start` value for `align-content`.

- Edit the CSS code:

```css
.container {
display: flex;
background-color: #f5ca3c;
flex-wrap: wrap;
height: 100vh;
align-content: flex-start;
}
```

With the default value for the `flex-direction` property (row), the value `flex-start` for the `align-content` property placex the wrapped lines at the top of the flex-container.

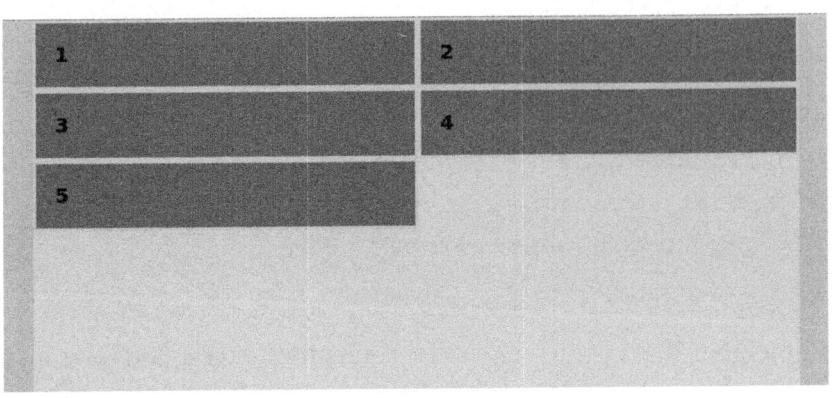

In the same manner, `align-content: flex-end` will place the wrapped lines at the bottom of the container.

- Edit the CSS code:

```
.container {
display: flex;
background-color: #f5ca3c;
flex-wrap: wrap;
height: 100vh;
align-content: flex-end;
}
```

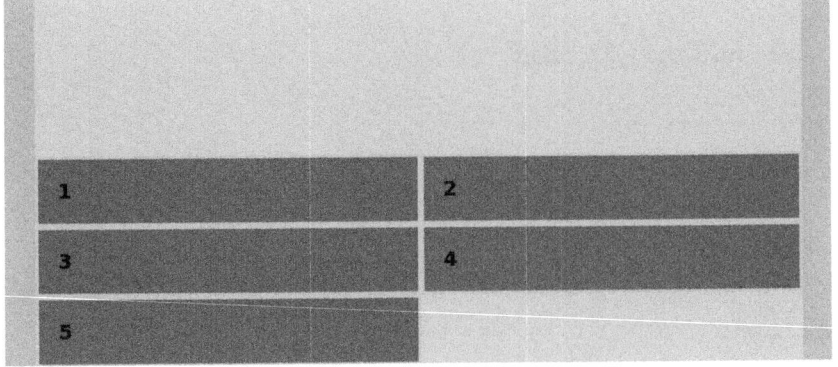

Moving on, let's test the `space-around` value for `align-content`.

- Edit the CSS code:

```
.container {
display: flex;
background-color: #f5ca3c;
flex-wrap: wrap;
height: 100vh;
align-content: space-around;
}
```

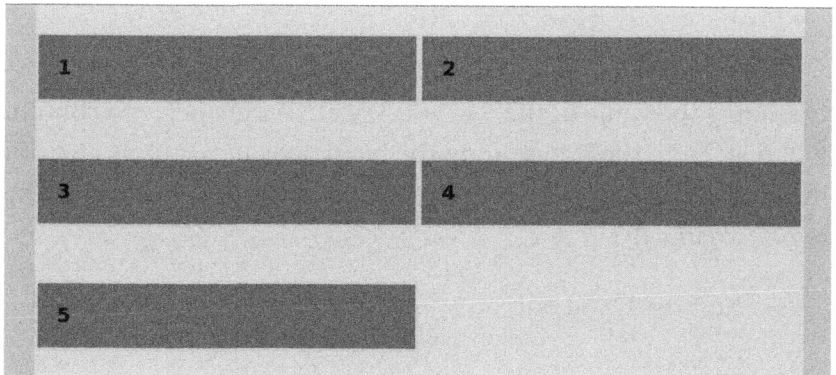

The `space-around` value tells the lines to take the available space in the container and divide it around them, whereas the `space-between` value places the first line at the top and the last line at the bottom of the container and then divides the available space between the lines.

- Edit the CSS code:

```
.container {
display: flex;
background-color: #f5ca3c;
flex-wrap: wrap;
height: 100vh;
```

```
align-content: space-between;
}
```

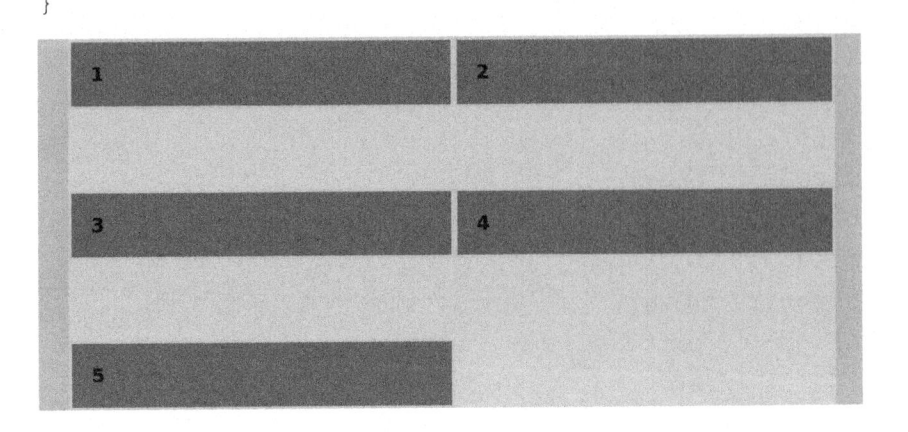

On the Block Axis

Changing the value of the `flex-direction` property to column will distribute the items along the block axis in columns and not in rows. That means that the lines will turn into columns. The logic remains the same.

- Edit the CSS code:

```
.container {
display: flex;
flex-direction: column;
background-color: #f5ca3c;
flex-wrap: wrap;
height: 100vh;
align-content: space-between;
}
```

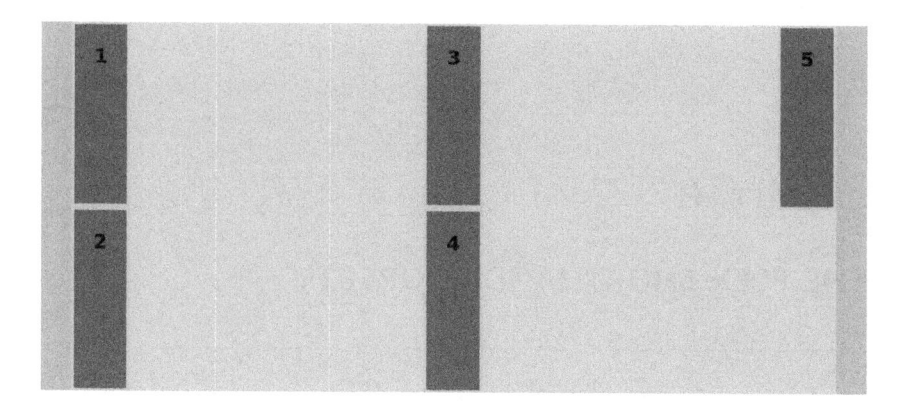

CHAPTER SUMMARY

The `align-content` property specifies how the lines inside the container will be distributed once you have applied the `flex-wrap` property. We tested six different values:

- `stretch` (default)
- `center`
- `flex-start`
- `flex-end`
- `space-around`
- `space-between`

In this chapter, we really got to build on top of our Flexbox knowledge. We combined what we've learned about several Flexbox properties,

In the final two chapters of the book, we'll keep combining concepts and digging into more advanced Flexbox techniques.

CHAPTER 11.

THE FLEX SHORTHAND PROPERTY

Before we start this chapter, let me remind you of three Flexbox properties we covered earlier in the book:

- `flex-grow` specifies how items expand to fill up the available remaining space within the flex-container.

- `flex-shrink` controls how items shrink if there is not enough space available within the flex-container.

- `flex-basis` assigns a fixed, ideal width or height to flex-items.

All of these properties can be summed up in one shorthand property, the `flex` property.

CREATE THE HTML AND CSS

- Open your preferred code editor.

- Create an empty HTML file.

- Copy this HTML code to your file: https://codepen.io/ jorgemb76/pen/MdLRXd.

- Create a file called style.css.

- Write this code, or copy it from the Codepen link above.

```
/* GLOBAL STYLES */
```

```
{
box-sizing: border-box;
}

body {
background-color: #AAA;
margin: 0px 50px 50px;
}

.item {
padding: 2rem;
border: 5px solid #87b5ff;
border-radius: 3px;
font-size: 2em;
font-family: sans-serif;
font-weight: bold;
background-color: #1c57b5;
}
```

This image shows the layout we have to start this chapter:

THE FLEXBOX STYLES

As always, before we go any further, let's declare the flex-container.

- Edit the CSS code:

```
.container {
display: flex;
background-color: #f5ca3c;
}
```

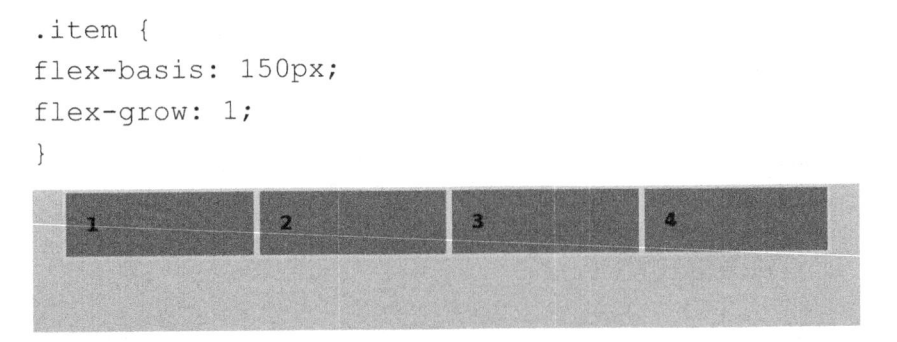

Each one of the items is a flex-item now. Use the `flex-basis` property in order to declare an initial "ideal" width for each flex-item.

- Edit the CSS code:

```
.item {
flex-basis: 150px;
}
```

Each one of the flex-items is 150px wide by default. However, there is uncovered space in the flex-container. To solve this, we use the `flex-grow` property.

- Edit the CSS code:

```
.item {
flex-basis: 150px;
flex-grow: 1;
}
```

Each one of the items takes the same amount of available space in proportion to its siblings.

When reaching a container width of less than 600px, the items will shrink proportionally to each other. That is because the flex-shrink property value is 1 by default. The layout will remain unchanged if you add this property-value pair to the code.

- Edit the CSS code:

```
.item {
flex-basis: 150px;
flex-grow: 1;
flex-shrink: 1;
}
```

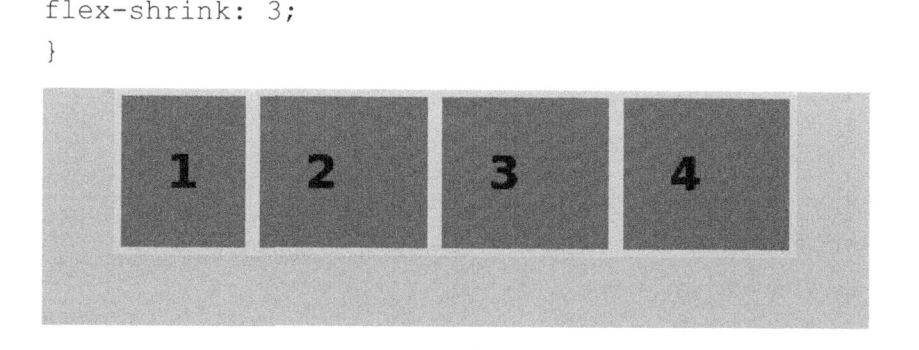

Target the first item and set its flex-shrink property to 3.

- Edit the CSS code:

```
.item1 {
flex-shrink: 3;
}
```

The flex Shorthand Property

The three properties assigned to the `.item` class can be shortened in one line using the `flex` shorthand property. You have to enter the values in this order:

1. `flex-grow`

2. `flex-shrink`

3. `flex-basis`

- Edit the CSS code:

```css
.item {
flex: 1 1 150px;
}
```

- Resize your browser window to test the code. You will see no difference in the layout. Your code on the other side seems much cleaner.

CHAPTER SUMMARY

If you haven't realized it already, we hope this chapter has shown you how clean and elegant Flexbox can be. With just a few characters, a line such as `flex: 1 1 150px;` gives us enormous control over our layouts.

In the final chapter of the book, we'll keep building on the concepts we've learned so far.

CHAPTER 12.

VALUES FOR THE FLEX SHORTHAND PROPERTY

In the previous chapter, you learned about the `flex` shorthand property. The flex property can group together three flexbox properties in the following order:

1. `flex-grow`
2. `flex-shrink`
3. `flex-basis`

The *flex* property can accept up to three value. However, you can enter only one or two values and the CSS Flexbox specification will assign the default missing value to the corresponding `flex` items.

CREATE THE HTML AND CSS

- Open your preferred code editor.
- Create an empty HTML file.
- Add this HTML code to your file: https://codepen.io/ jorgemb76/pen/MMbozg.
- Create a file called style.css.
- Write this CSS code, or copy-and-paste from the Codepen link above.

```
/* GLOBAL STYLES */
{
box-sizing: border-box;
}

body {
background-color: #AAA;
margin: 0px 50px 50px;
}

.item {
padding: 2rem;
border: 5px solid #87b5ff;
border-radius: 3px;
font-size: 2em;
font-family: sans-serif;
font-weight: bold;
background-color: #1c57b5;
}
```

CREATE THE FLEXBOX STYLES

One last time in this book, let's declare the `flex` container:

- Edit the CSS code:

```
.container {
display: flex;
```

```
background-color: #f5ca3c;
}
```

The `.container` element is now a `flex` container. All its direct children have turned into `flex` items at the same time.

THE FLEX PROPERTY DEFAULTS

You have to apply the `flex` shorthand property to one, some or all the `flex` items inside the container. As you already know, you can use one, two or three values here.

One-Value Syntax

The one-value syntax can accept a couple of value types:

- a number – it will be interpreted as `flex-grow`
- a valid keyword – `initial`, `auto` or `none`.

Open your text editor in order to test these value types.

- Edit the CSS code:

```
.item {
flex: 1;
}
```

You set the `flex-grow` factor of every item to 1. That means every item will grow in equal proportion to fill up the available space.

- Edit the CSS code:

```
.item {
flex: auto;
}
```

Items will grow and shrink with a factor of 1. The flex-basis value is auto.

- Edit the CSS code:

```
.item {
flex: initial;
}
```

This is the same as flex: 0 1 auto; – items have a flex-grow factor of 0. They do not grow to fill up the available space; however, they will shrink in the same proportion, in case that there is not enough space available.

- Edit the CSS code:

```
.item {
flex: none;
}
```

The items are fully inflexible. They will not be able to grow or shrink relative to the flex container. This would be the same as typing flex: 0 0 auto;

TWO-VALUE SYNTAX

The two value syntax can accept:

- two numbers – interpreted as `flex-grow` + `flex-shrink`

- a number and a width value – interpreted as `flex-grow` + `flex-basis`

Edit the CSS file once again:

```
.item {
flex: 0 2;
}
```

In this case, you set the `flex-grow` factor to 0 and the `flex-shrink` factor to 2. The `flex-grow` factor of 0 means that items will not grow to fill the available space. The `flex-shrink` factor of 2 means that all items will shrink in the same proportion to accommodate themselves into the available space if there wasn't enough.

- Edit the CSS one last time:

```
.item {
flex: 0 150px;
}
```

Now every item has a `flex-grow` factor of 0, and a `flex-basis` value of 150px.

FLEXBOX SUMMARY

Thank you so much for following Flexbox Explained all the way through to the end.

We wish you all the best with your webdesign work, and hope that you'll find many uses for Flexbox.

If you have any questions, we're here for you: books@ostraining.com.

Jorge and Steve

Made in United States
Orlando, FL
16 July 2022

19877078R00055